In *15 Powerfu...*
has developed some ... ... into a set
of practical tools to help you understand your child
better so that you can help your child reach her or his full potential.

Modesty

Courtesy

Integrity

Perseverance

Courage

Indomitable Spirit

Hello!

WHETHER YOU ARE A NEW PARENT or a child psychologist with ten children of your own, *15 Powerful Tools for Successful Parenting* was written for you.

I'm proud to say that, as a professional martial arts instructor, I have taught or supervised the instruction of nearly twenty thousand children over the course of more than thirty years. A lot of the tools in *15 Powerful Tools for Successful Parenting* come right off the mat.

Through my interaction with students and their parents over the years, I've had the privilege of seeing great parenting in action. Before having children of my own, I interviewed dozens of parents whom I felt were doing a great job in order to learn strategies that I could put to use.

In this quest to enhance my teaching skills, I have read literally hundreds of books on teaching, coaching and parenting. During my research, I came across a broad spectrum of parenting strategies, some of which were diametrically opposed to one another. However, certain concepts were consistent throughout my research. *15 Powerful Tools for Successful Parenting* weaves these common threads into a logical, concise and easy-to-read guide to being a great parent.

I've been applying these principles both to my parenting and martial arts instruction for decades and they're as useful now as they ever were.

I hope you have a great time teaming up with your child to use the tools in *15 Powerful Tools for Successful Parenting*.

And please note that I refer to your child as either "he" or "she" throughout the book to simplify the message, but all the tools apply to both sons and daughters.

Happy parenting!

Dave Kovar

Your Most Important Role *6*

Guideline 1: Praise in public, but reprimand in private *8*

Guideline 2: Believe in your child's potential *12*

Guideline 3: Walk your talk *18*

Guideline 4: Constantly catch your child "doing things right" *22*

Guideline 5: Set boundaries and stick to them *26*

Guideline 6: Listen *32*

Guideline 7: Hold your children to a high standard *36*

Guideline 8: Inspire your child to greatness *40*

Guideline 9: Choose your battles wisely *44*

Guideline 10: Be easily in awe *50*

Guideline 11: Give your child choices, not ultimatums *54*

Guideline 12: Never compare *60*

Guideline 13: Maintain *rigid flexibility* *66*

Guideline 14: Don't speak out of anger *72*

Guideline 15: Make sure your child knows that you love her unconditionally *78*

Why Your Child Needs Martial Arts *84*

Keeping It Simple *86*

About the Author *88*

Your Most Important Role

THE MOST IMPORTANT ROLE YOU WILL EVER HAVE is that of parent. Parenting can be extremely rewarding, but it's extremely challenging, too. Just when you think you have it figured out, something happens and it's back to the drawing board.

Ben Zoma, an early spiritual sage, often asked his students, "Who is a brave person?" Zoma described "a brave person" as "someone who is smart enough to be afraid, but does whatever needs to be done anyway."

To me, "being afraid" means that certain things are to be taken seriously. Parenthood is a real responsibility. Like it or not, we're responsible for helping to shape our child's life. We should not take this lightly.

Sow a thought, reap an action.
Sow an action, reap a habit.
Sow a habit, reap a character.
Sow a character, reap a destiny.

The above quote, attributed to Ralph Waldo Emerson, is one of my favorites. First and foremost, a parent's job is to do his best to raise his child to become a confident, healthy, happy and contributing member of society. And, in order to do this, parents need to help their children think in proactive, positive ways and develop strong self-images that will guide them through rough times.

The following *Parenting Guidelines* are designed to support your and your child's success.

You have probably heard most of these guidelines before. Most of them are common sense. However, knowing *what* to do and understanding *how* to do it are often two separate challenges. *15 Powerful Tools for Successful Parenting* unites the *what* with the *how* for a logical, easy-to-use guide to parenting.

As you read, you might think that I'm exaggerating the importance of being positive with your child. Guilty as charged! In my experience of working with thousands of parents over the course of more than thirty years, rarely have I come across parents who are too positive with their children. I have, however, frequently seen parents spend way too much time criticizing and being negative with their children. At the other end of this spectrum, though more rare, are parents who believe their children can do no wrong. Both approaches are off kilter.

15 Powerful Tools for Successful Parenting teaches positive, logical and effective parenting and communication skills in an intuitive format so that you will be able to begin to apply them immediately.

We're all busy. Even with the best of intentions, days or weeks might slip by in which we haven't used any of our parenting tools. If these tools make sense to you, you might try calendaring them into your phone or computer, even setting the alarm clock on your phone as a reminder or writing yourself notes placed in strategic locations.

Guideline 1

Praise in public, but reprimand in private.

There is no better feeling than public recognition from someone we respect. We should be constantly looking for opportunities to praise our children openly.

Praise

Appreciation

Celebration

Encouragement

Respect

Dignity

Description

Don't miss any opportunity to let your child know he did a great job. Rewarding him in the moment is the way to encourage his great attitude and excellent effort.

Most of us have experienced public humiliation sometime in our life. For many people, these memories haunt them forever. Being a parent is not easy. Sometimes we get angry and want to "teach our child a lesson." But it's important to remember that, no matter how angry we are or what our child has done, we should not humiliate or reprimand him in front of others. The best way is to cool down first and then address the matter privately.

A Great Example

Sensei Bruce was my first karate teacher. He is a good guy and I'm happy to say that, forty years later, we're still in touch. Back in those days, not a lot of children took martial arts and there was no thought put into teaching methodology. Public praise and positive reinforcement were not in Sensei Bruce's arsenal. As a matter fact, I don't think I ever heard him say anything positive about me during those first couple of years training. It wasn't that he was rude or mean, he just didn't think to give any of his students any positive feedback.

One day, my father came into the school to pick me up. He was a bit early, so he sat down for a few moments to watch the remaining part of class. Unbeknownst to me, Sensei Bruce had decided to promote me to blue belt at the close of class. In front of the class and my father, he said aloud, "Dave, he's a tiger. He is doing great and could be a champion someday. Tonight I'm awarding him his blue belt. He certainly deserves it." I can't tell you how amazing it made me feel to have my instructor tell my dad and the rest of class that I was doing so well. I was on cloud nine the whole way home. I've never forgotten that incident. It reminds me to pass on public praise to my children and my students whenever possible.

Room for Improvement

When I was young, I was at a party at my friend's house where there were dozens of guests of all ages. After dinner, all the kids were told to rinse their plates off and put them in the dishwasher. My friend forgot to do this and left his dish on the counter. Seeing this, his father jumped at the chance to "teach him a lesson." In front of everyone, he berated his son. I'll never forget my friend's pain and embarrassment at being publicly humiliated.

Tool 1: Like Indiana Jones, go on a treasure hunt. But you're not looking for an ark. You're searching for opportunities to praise your child during your normal, daily activities. These moments could occur at the grocery store, social gatherings, talking with friends on the phone, or just about anywhere where you and your child are with other people. It might take practice but praising your child in public will soon come naturally.

Guideline 2

Believe in your child's potential.

Probably the single most important factor that will increase your child's overall success in life is your own belief that she can succeed.

Belief
Expectancy
Vision
Conviction

Description

Your belief in your child's potential is very powerful. As parents, we need to know and believe that our children have the ability to succeed. Then we must act accordingly. Amazing things will happen.

A Great Example

I remember TJ as we'd met yesterday. This young boy was from India. TJ was very bright, but terribly shy and quite possibly the most uncoordinated child that I had ever taught. After his first introductory lesson, his father asked me point blank, "What do you think? Can he ever be any good at this? Do you think he can ever be a Black Belt?" Not wanting to disappoint the father or lower TJ's self esteem more than it already was, I lied. I told them that, although it would be difficult, I had complete faith in TJ and I knew that, if he stuck it out, he would one day earn his Black Belt. The father responded by saying, "Well, you're the expert. If you believe that he can do it, that is good enough for me. Let's get him signed up."

The guilt started the moment they left and continued to build to the point that I was sick to my stomach. I had completely sold out. There was NO way in this lifetime that TJ would ever even earn his yellow belt, let alone his Black Belt. How could I mislead this nice family? Tim, my brother and business partner, was able to calm me down a bit by reminding me that TJ had nowhere to go but up and that our program would help even him.

I decided to make helping TJ succeed my personal project. I made sure to give him a lot of attention and encouragement. Over time, a funny thing began to happen... TJ started to get it and, before long, he successfully passed his yellow belt test.

Five years later, I found him in front of me, amongst a group of newly promoted Junior Black Belts. He had done it and quite well at that! After the test, he and his dad asked to speak privately with me. The father began express his appreciation for the program and how much it had done for TJ. Then TJ said, "Thanks for believing in me. I never thought I could do it, but you were so sure that I could and I didn't want to let you down."

TJ continued to train for a few more years. He grew into a fine young man. The last time we talked, he was in medical school. I've lost touch with him now, but I hope our paths will cross again because I never really got the chance to thank him. Looking back, I realize that I learned way more from TJ than he ever learned from me. He taught me how to be a better teacher. He showed me what perseverance really is. Most importantly, he demonstrated the power of believing in someone.

Room for Improvement

Early on in my career, I attended a Zig Zigler seminar. At this seminar, I heard him share a statistic about inmates in the Texas State Penitentiary. He said that over fifty-percent of the inmates were told by their parents when they were young that they would end up in prison.

While an interesting statistic, I didn't fully believe it until I saw firsthand this exact thing happen. Daniel was ten years old when he and his sister enrolled in our martial arts school. Both were good children, but it was clear that they had a hard life. Their grandmother was raising them. Over time, I found out that their dad was an alcoholic and a drug addict with whom they barely had contact. Their mother was incarcerated and wouldn't be eligible for parole for several years.

I saw their dad only one time. He came into the school to watch them compete in a small tournament. It was obvious that Daniel wanted to do well for his father. When he won his match, I heard his dad say, "It is going to take a lot more than that to impress me, Danny. You'll probably wind up just like your mother." I've never been so close to kicking someone in my life! Okay, I've kicked lots of people. I'm a martial artist. But only in training, never in anger.

Daniel and Sarah trained with me for years after that incident. Eventually, they drifted away from the school. Later, I learned from Sarah that Daniel was doing time for car theft.

I know that Daniel and Sarah's parents were extreme, but still, there's a lesson to be learned from them. Every now and then, I drive by the house

Daniel and Sarah lived in when I knew them. After my thoughts wander to Daniel and where he might be now, they return to my children in the present. You can be sure that the next conversation I have with my children will be one in which I affirm their potential.

Tool 2: Every morning as you are brushing your teeth, ask yourself if your words and actions have been congruent with your belief in your child's potential. If not, decide how you will affirm your child's potential that day.

Guideline 3

Walk your talk.

Children pay attention to everything we do as parents. What we do has a far greater impact on our children than what we say.

Leadership
Integrity
Honesty
Example
Consistency

Description

When we live and act honestly and in keeping with our own integrity without compromise, we set the best example for our children. We keep our eye on the big picture—our own integrity and the character development of our children—rather than compromise our integrity and honesty for short-term gain.

A Great Example

I remember being in line with my father to buy tickets for a movie one time when I was a kid. I was fourteen years old, but I looked about eleven. I mentioned to my father that if he said I was twelve, we could save a couple of bucks off the price of admission. I had a friend whose father did that all the time and it seemed like a logical thing to do. I will never forget what happened next. He looked at me and said, "My honesty is worth a whole lot more than the two dollars I'll save from lying about your age." I still hear those words repeated in my head every time I think about cutting a corner.

Room for Improvement

I am always learning how to be a better parent. However much I try to be a good example for my children, I still end up being a hypocrite sometimes. A great example of this was when my son was taking Driver's Ed. I hadn't realized how many basic driving rules that I was breaking until he reminded me. It's lucky he wasn't a highway patrolman because I would have lost my license for sure.

At first, I used the excuse that I had been driving for thirty-five years and I know what I'm doing. Not only did he not buy it, but I felt totally hypocritical saying it. So I decided that the best thing that I could do for my son was to do a better job in following the rules of the road.

Tool 3: List three ways that you can be a better example to your child. Then follow through and implement them.

Guideline 4

Constantly catch your child "doing things right."

When you are in the habit of catching your child doing things right, you reinforce appropriate behavior. Everything goes better.

Alertness
Observation
Appreciation
Reinforcement

Description

Most of us don't need to be reminded to correct our children when they are messing up, because we do that enough already. However, we do need to look out for what our children do right and, when we see something, make sure to tell them about it.

Unfortunately, following kids around and showing them everything they don't do so well is quite common with parents. Upper and lower income, functional and dysfunctional families, it doesn't seem to matter. "Let me show you another thing that you did wrong" seems to be a common parenting technique.

A Great Example

I have a friend of mine who utilizes praise as a parenting strategy unwaveringly. He makes a point to catch his children doing things right. He looks for something that each of his children did right everyday—a neat, well-done homework assignment, putting the dirty clothes in the hamper, or loading the dishwasher after dinner.

Of course, he still corrects his children and makes suggestions when needed but those corrections and suggestions are easier for his children to swallow because of all the good stuff he's catching them doing.

Room for Improvement

As a child, I spent a lot of time down the street at the Gray's house. They had a pool, a billiards table and a whole lot of ice cream in the freezer. The only drawback was Mrs. Gray. All the kids referred to her as the "neighborhood nag." She was constantly on both of her boys and, for that matter, her boys' friends. Nothing was ever done well enough to suit her. She constantly found fault.

One day, Mr. Gray asked his sons and me to clean up the kitchen before Mrs. Gray got home. We went to it, almost excited as we anticipated Mrs. Gray's compliment on a job well done. Upon her return, the boys raced out to meet her, excited to show her what we had accomplished.

Instead of appreciating our efforts, she complained that the floor hadn't been swept and the garbage had not been emptied. I remained friends with the Gray boys for years to come. I didn't see them try to please their mother after that incident. After all, pleasing her was impossible. Why even try?

Over the years, their relationship with their mother continued to deteriorate until, last I heard, they no longer had contact with her. I know she loved her boys but in her attempt to "make them better" she never praised their efforts or caught them doing things right.

Mrs. Gray taught me a lot of what not to do as a parent. Correcting my children is necessary at times, but I spend more time looking for what they're doing right. The more I look, the more I discover.

Tool 4: Everyday, make it a point to catch your child doing at least three things right.

Guideline 5

Set boundaries
and stick to them.

Children like to know where the boundaries are, even when they complain about them. Boundaries make them feel safe.

Clarity

Consistency

Firmness

Fairness

Consequences

Safety

Description

Your child is going to test the boundaries. That's his job but if you set realistic boundaries and stick to them, things usually work out pretty well.

Don't be too quick to set boundaries to which you will not or cannot adhere. Suggestions and encouragement are a great source of motivation. However, when they don't work and it's necessary to set clear boundaries, do so and don't deviate from the boundaries you set.

A Great Example

We used to take a lot of road trips as a family when I was a kid. All five of us would hop into the family compact car and head off for a family vacation, which was usually at least six states away. These trips always started out fine. We were a little cramped in the car, but had fun just the same. Most evenings we would camp out. Rarely would it be in an official campsite. Usually it was on a frontage road just off the highway. My dad's philosophy was to make good time, drive until you're dead tired and then pull over anywhere, throw the sleeping bags down and call it a night.

Usually, we'd get to stay one night in a motel as a special treat. This was a big deal for us. Generally it was the middle of summer. We had no air conditioning. There were five of us stuffed into a four-seater. We were all excited by the thought of swimming in the motel pool and enjoying the luxury of beds, my dad included.

On one trip, we were driving from California to Minnesota to see relatives. On the third day of the trip, my dad announced that it would be "motel night" that night. By this time, we three children were restless and pretty tired of each other. The teasing started and went on for hours. My mom and dad asked us to quit fighting several times but we had had it and weren't listening. Finally, my dad had had enough and laid down some strong boundaries. He told us that we would drive straight through to Minneapolis instead of stopping at a motel if we didn't shape up. We calmed down for a few moments but I don't think any of us really believed him. He gave us one last warning but we still didn't listen.

True to his word, my dad drove all night and halfway into the next day until we arrived in Minneapolis. It was a rough night and one I didn't forget. Needless to say, we got the point. On our return trip to California, we shaped up when he asked us to because we knew he'd stick to his boundaries. And yes, that motel pool in Wells, Nevada was the best swim ever!

Room for Improvement

Several years ago, my wife and I had were dining in a nice restaurant when I was startled by a rather loud, authoritative voice behind me saying, "If you don't eat all your peas, you can't have any dessert."

I glanced over my shoulder to see a young couple and their 5-year old daughter. The father's statement had caught my attention and I was curious as to how events would unfold. The couple's daughter obviously didn't like peas and she let her parents know that.

Pretty soon I heard, "Eat half of your peas and you can have dessert," followed minutes later by, "You need to eat at least one spoonful of peas if you want dessert." Shortly there after, I saw the waiter replace a plate full of peas with a big bowl of ice cream.

I'm not sure how many peas the little girl ate but my guess is not many. This young couple loved their daughter. They were trying their best to be good parents. The problem was that, if they continued to set boundaries with their daughter but failed to keep them, they would eventually become powerless as parents.

I was especially intrigued by this event because my daughter was the same age at the time. It made me wonder if my wife and I ever did the same thing with our children and that, perhaps, we were just not aware of it. The two of us talked it over and decided that, although we were probably not nearly as bad as the couple we had witnessed at dinner, we could do better.

We decided that, when boundaries did need to be set, we'd do so and that not even an act of Congress would be able to get us to move them.

Tool 5: Decide if the boundaries you have currently set for your child are realistic. If they aren't, adjust them. Make sure that everyone in the house knows what the rules are and what the consequences are for breaking them. Be firm but fair.

Guideline 6

Listen.

Listening is the key to all great relationships. One of the best ways to build a healthy relationship with your child is to listen to him. By listening, you show your child you care and respect him. By listening, you show your child the meaning of the words, "I love you."

Openness

Curiosity

Interest

Attention

Calm

Respect

Non-reaction

Description

Listening to your children seems pretty obvious. "Hearing" and "listening" are quite different, though. We often "hear" the words coming out of our children's mouths, but how often do we really "listen" to what our children are saying?

Listening means that you are interested in what's going on in your child's life. Constantly remind your child that you are there for him and that he can talk to you about anything. Tell your child that, although you might not always like what he has to say, you are always there for him.

A Great Example

Dana and her husband Scott are close family friends. Dana has a quality that I rarely see. She is the most amazing listener. It doesn't matter what the topic of conversation is. She takes a genuine interest in other people and their lives. People feel smart, funny and appreciated around Dana and want to share their lives with her. She listens without judgment. Good or bad, it doesn't matter. She listens. Our children have noticed it, too. She's a great example of what I constantly strive to do better with my children…to really listen.

Room for Improvement

My daughter and I were going for a walk. She was telling me about her school day in detail, but my mind was somewhere else. Finally, in the middle of a sentence she stepped in front of me, looked me in the eye and said, "Dad, be in the moment. You aren't even listening to me." Of course she was absolutely right and it wasn't the first time that she caught me being mentally checked out. I apologized and brought my attention back to the present moment. We had a great conversation and I really appreciated being able to share that moment with her.

Tool 6: Take at least a few minutes everyday to listen to your child with complete focus and without judgment, comment or correction. Sometimes "conversation" doesn't include much talking. Basically just relax and listen.

Guideline 7

Hold your children to a high standard.

It's amazing what children can accomplish when they set their minds to it and are encouraged to do their best by people they respect. "Whether the task be big or small, do it right or not at all." I remember learning this phrase from my grandmother years ago.

Expectations

Diligence

Discipline

Integrity

Effort

Fairness

Accountability

Description

Holding your child to a high standard can be taken to extremes. As parents, we can certainly go too far and demand either too much or too little from our children. So how do you know for sure how hard to push your child or how much to expect from her? Parenting is more of an art than a science, so we'll never know for sure. The most important thing to do is to evaluate each situation individually.

A Great Example

I remember a moment one summer when my grandmother called me to task after inspecting the mediocre job I had done mowing their backyard. She very nicely told me that I was capable of doing much better. She explained to me that my grandfather would be home within an hour and that there was plenty of time left to get the job done right. So, I begrudgingly stepped up my game. You know what? It felt pretty good when my grandfather raved about how the lawn had never looked better and what a great job I had done. My grandmother winked at me. We shared a secret that afternoon and, to this day, I'm better for it.

Room for Improvement

Early on in my career, I had a young student named Johnny. Just after Johnny enrolled, his mom pulled me aside to let me know that Johnny had some learning disabilities and couldn't be expected to progress at the same rate as other kids. She asked me if I would be patient with him and not push him too hard.

Of course, I agreed and Johnny's training began. It was a good thing that I didn't push him too hard because he was progressing slower than other children...or so I thought. A few months into his training I took a week's vacation and had one of my senior students teach Johnny's class for me. Tom was eager and had a good knack for working with young children, but he was inexperienced.

In my excitement to leave for vacation I forgot to tell Tom that he should take it easy on Johnny. I thought nothing of this until my flight home. My heart began to race as I envisioned getting a lecture from Johnny's mom about her son being pushed too hard. Even worse yet, I imagined Johnny experiencing humiliation because he could not keep up with the rest of the class while I was gone.

Much to my surprise, I returned to find Johnny performing at a much higher level than I had thought possible. He was proud of his new skills and so was his mother. What had changed while I had been gone? Tom had no preconceived ideas of Johnny's limitations. Therefore, he held him to a higher standard and Johnny happily rose to the occasion.

Tool 7: Ask yourself these questions—Is it realistic for me to expect more of my child here? If so, how much? For this situation, what is the best way to encourage my child to do better?

Guideline 8

Inspire your child
to greatness.

In most cases, parents are the most influential people in a child's life. Therefore, it is very important that you try to make your interactions with your child as positive and uplifting as possible.

Opportunity

Positivity

Communication

Confidence

Expectation

Completion

Success

Description

Every day is filled with opportunities to plant positive seeds in your child's mind. Children (especially young children) are blank canvases waiting to be painted. You can give your child a new way to think about how he views himself. And you can literally put new words in your child's head for him to use later.

Rather than being disappointed in or critical of your child, you can turn the situation into a challenge for him to perform at a higher level. Even though he might feel as if he is facing an insurmountable difficulty, show him that he can overcome obstacles and still function. With repetition, your child will begin to know that he can do what is required, even when it isn't easy. For example, your child might think, "I don't feel like doing my homework today, but my dad expects me to do it because he knows that I can do it even when I'm tired."

So, instead of falling prey to sympathizing or agreeing with your child's diminished view of himself, be sure to build up your child's confidence and inspire him to greatness.

A Great Example

A friend of mine has four children, all of them bright, grounded and happy. I asked him what his basic viewpoints on parenting were and I was not a bit surprised to hear his answer.

He said, "I constantly remind them how smart and capable they are and how proud I am of all the hard work and effort they put into all of their activities. And I make sure to tell them this even before they start a new project."

Room for Improvement

As a child, I played baseball for a few seasons. Coach Coursey, was my friend's dad and a good guy with the best of intentions. During the summer of my last season, I was at the Coursey's house playing with my friend. The coach came out and we had a nice talk about baseball, our last season and the future. Then he definitively told me that I wasn't very good at team sports, but was better at individual sports.

At the time, I accepted Coach Coursey's comment as fact. I excelled at sports I perceived to be "individual" sports. Because I respected Coach Coursey, I believed what he said to be true. After that season, I didn't pursue team sports. Instead, I excelled at wrestling, skiing and karate. Later I realized that martial arts, a sport I perceived to be an individual sport, is very much a team sport. The coach was unaware of the impact of his words on me.

As an adult, I've learned that I am a pretty good team player after all. However, Coach Coursey's one statement that summer afternoon years ago had a profound effect on my belief system which took me literally decades to undo.

Tool 8: Remind your child of how capable he is at least twice everyday. Constantly affirm him, believe in him and let him feel his own potential. Be delighted that he's dreaming big. And never make him feel foolish for having such big dreams.

Guideline 9

Choose your battles wisely.

Sometimes, you just have to let your child be. Sometimes, you just have to look the other direction. Of course, with issues of safety or morality, you should address the issue promptly. But when you're dealing with less important issues, remember always to choose your battles wisely.

Flexibility

Openness

Prioritizing

Humanity

Compassion

Ease

Description

Pope John Paul II was once asked what the best way was to get along with others. He replied, "See everything, overlook a lot, and correct a little." This is great advice! It's applicable to every type of relationship but especially to the parent-child relationship.

We probably all know someone who endlessly nitpicks at his child. That someone might even be us. We all want to help our children be all that they can be. Constantly correcting them might seem logical but this strategy almost always has the reverse effect on children.

Excessive exposure to negative comments only strengthens your child's need to protect himself and defy you. To be excessively concerned with or critical of inconsequential details creates distance between you and your child. Nobody's perfect and your child is no exception. Why, then, nitpick?

If you are on him about everything, pretty soon he won't listen to you regarding anything. The day you are able to resist commenting on his mismatched wardrobe or shaggy haircut, the fact that he left his socks in the living room, his talking with his mouth full, or that the slang he uses isn't proper English, is probably the day that he will be more receptive to whatever important input you do give him.

A Great Example

Growing up, my father was relatively lenient compared to some of my friends' dads. Maybe he could afford to be lenient because my brother, sister and I weren't real big troublemakers. Sure, we got into trouble from time to time and we didn't always get along but overall our parents didn't need to resort to strict discipline. I felt my parents were pretty reasonable people. I was given plenty of freedom as long as my attitude was right and my grades stayed decent.

My father had a motorcycle when he was growing up. He used to tell us about his experiences riding (mostly in disbelief that his dad let him have a bike in the first place because of all the dumb things that he did). He told my brother and me more than once that he didn't feel motorcycles should be in our future.

I wanted one, however. So when I had a chance to buy a motorcycle from a friend at a bargain price at age seventeen, I jumped at the chance. As I was driving it home for the first time, I imagined the conversation that my father and I would have. I wasn't too concerned. I knew that, eventually, I would be able to talk him into letting me keep it.

Upon first glance, my father looked at me and, in a stern voice, he said, "Nice bike. Sell it." Then he reached out and took the keys from me. My first ride on that motorcycle was also my last. I didn't question his decision. I didn't try to change his mind. I knew in that one instant that motorcycle riding was nonnegotiable.

Room for Improvement

When my son was in grade school, I volunteered when I could and went on virtually every field trip from kindergarten to sixth grade. Over the years, I got to know the kids and their parents pretty well.

There is always a troublemaker or two in every school and my son's school was no different. Seth was one of these. A difficult child to like, Seth was constantly doing the wrong things for the wrong reasons.

Dealing with Seth's dad wasn't much easier. Seth's dad was ruthless in his parenting. He constantly argued and found fault with Seth, even when he didn't deserve it. One particular incident stands out in my mind.

I was carpooling for a day trip to a museum in Berkeley and Seth was in my car. We got along pretty well and he wasn't much trouble that day. When I dropped him off back at school, his dad was waiting for him. He walked up to the car and said, "Okay, what did Seth do today that I should know about?"

I responded by telling his father that Seth had a good day and I had nothing negative to report. At that moment, his father looked over at Seth (who had been eating Cheetos the whole way home and was covered with orange Cheetos goo) and chewed him out for being dirty. I can't help but think that Seth's challenges were due, at least in part, to his father's abrasiveness, relentlessness and inability to choose his battles wisely.

Tool 9: Make a list of all the things that you currently nitpick your child about. Decide which of these things you are willing to tolerate for now and then commit yourself to the concept of looking the other way when you see them happening. Finally, for every one thing that you decide to correct your child on, make it a habit to find at least one other thing (and, preferably, two) to praise him for.

Guideline 10

Be easily in awe.

Make the decision to allow yourself to be impressed often by your child. Being easily in awe is really about appreciating the time and effort your child puts into a project. And it's about letting her know how great she did.

Joy
Amazement
Receptivity
Delight

Description

Your child needs your approval and wants you to be impressed when she has done something well.

I am not talking about **false praise**, which can have a detrimental effect. **False praise** comes in many forms and usually we give it when we are not paying attention. For example, when your daughter shows you the finger painting she did in kindergarten, false praise might sound like a quick, "That's nice," as you carry on with your business.

Instead take a minute to pay attention and admire her artwork. Sincere praise resonates and might sound like, "Wow, I love it! There's a lot of blue here. You must really like blue. I really like how you mixed the blue with red to make purple. Can I put this on the refrigerator so everyone can see my daughter-the-artist's latest project? Keep up the great work. I'm proud of you."

Although you might quickly forget the interaction, your child will not. Your kind words will be ingrained on her psyche for years and will probably become part of her belief system for the rest of her life.

A Great Example

When I was in sixth grade, my teacher, Mrs. Austin, had the students write a book report and give an oral presentation on that same book. I don't remember what book I chose, but I do remember the conversation I had with Mrs. Austin directly after giving my oral report. She pulled me aside and said, "Wow, Dave, that was really good! You have excellent comprehension."

I'm sure Mrs. Austin wouldn't remember this conversation, but it's embedded in my psyche forever. To this day, I pride myself in having good comprehension. I have complete confidence that I will understand whatever I read very well. Why? Because Mrs. Austin told me that I have good comprehension, that's why.

Room for Improvement

When my son, Alex, was little, I came home from work in a big hurry because I wanted to go for a run before it got dark. My son was excited to show me his drawing of a dinosaur. I quickly walked over to the kitchen table and said blandly, "That's nice, son." Then I hurried to the bedroom to change for my run. A minute later, my wife walked into the bedroom and, by the look on her face, I knew I was in trouble. She told me that Alex had spent all afternoon drawing the dinosaur picture just for me and that he had asked her several times if he thought I would like it. My response wasn't what he had expected. He was disappointed that he wasn't the artist he thought he was. I mean after all, his dad hardly looked at it.

Of course, I went back out into the kitchen and reexamined Alex's drawing in detail. I would be a bit late for my run, but that was a small price to pay. I really paid attention and sincerely told him how wonderful it was. Although my belated response certainly helped, it would have helped a lot more if I had been in awe of him the first time. How much more time would that have taken? Thirty seconds! I vowed to do a better job of being easily in awe after that experience.

Tool 10: Be impressed by your child at least once everyday and then let her know.

Guideline 11

★

Give your child choices,
not ultimatums.

Give your child choices, rather than ultimatums, to empower him to take action to resolve the problem. You may think that giving an ultimatum keeps you in control of your child, but the reverse is true. And every time you don't follow up on an ultimatum, you lose credibility with him.

Choices
Logic
Calm
Control
Breath
Clarity
Empowerment

Description

A very common parental response to a misbehaving child is "the ultimatum." For example, "If you don't stop bothering your sister we are leaving Disneyland immediately and driving straight home." Giving this ultimatum can feel momentarily satisfying, but you'll usually regret it soon afterwards because you know that you won't follow through. And therein lies the problem. Your child knows that, too.

Logic and emotion are like oil and water. They don't mix. When we become emotional, we don't think clearly. We are likely to say and do things that we really don't mean. The next time you find yourself about to issue your child an ultimatum, stop and take a few deep breaths instead.

When your child is acting out, take a moment to breathe deeply and calm down. You'll be more likely to see the issue for what it is and respond more logically in a way that better fits the situation. You will be able to give your child appropriate choices to empower him to take action to resolve the situation.

Then you can give your child options. For example, "Would you like to do your homework now or in 15 minutes?" Or "Do you want broccoli or spinach with your sandwich?" Likewise, "Do you want to come home at 7 or 7:30 p.m.?"

This makes your child feel more in control. When you give him a choice, you are more likely to get his cooperation.

A Great Example

The Connors' children and ours grew up together. Our families were good friends and did a lot together. The Connors' youngest boy, Nicholas, came into this world testing their patience. Their older two children were incredibly well-behaved and easy, so this third child really threw them for a loop. Nicholas constantly pushed limits.

One night over dinner, young Nicholas threw peas at his big brother. This wasn't the first incident of the evening for him and I could tell that his dad was losing patience. Instead of saying, "If you don't stop that immediately, I will lock you in the closet for a week," like I sensed he wanted to, his father took a deep breath and said calmly, "Nicholas, if you stop now you can still have dessert and watch the movie with the other kids after dinner. If you don't stop immediately, you'll be done for the night and you'll get neither. It's your choice."

Because his father had followed through in the past, Nicholas knew that the consequences were real and that he had a decision to make. Nicholas made a good choice and behaved for the rest of the evening. I know it doesn't always happen like that, but it only took this one incident for me to see the value of giving choices and not ultimatums.

Room for Improvement

The checkout line at the grocery store was long. There had to have been at least four people in front of me, all with extremely full carts. The man in front of me had two small children and was doing his best control them, but with very little success. I quickly got the impression that he was at a loss as to how to handle his kids.

Soon the ultimatums began. The first one was, "If you two don't calm down immediately, you are going to be in so much trouble when we get home." That one worked for all of ten seconds.

Next the father pulled the box of Popsicles from the cart and threatened to put them back. His two children stared at him blankly for a moment and then resumed their arguing. By the way, the Popsicles stayed in the cart even after the ultimatum. When that didn't work the dad lost it and yelled, "That's it! You're grounded for a month, both of you!"

I could tell that his words were empty and that he probably would not follow through. And guess what? I'm pretty sure his children knew he wouldn't, as well. Of course, that father loved his children and was doing his best to control them. Unfortunately, no one ever explained to him the importance of giving choices with logical consequences instead of ultimatums.

Tool 11: Think of an ongoing challenge that you're currently facing with your child. Decide on some options that you can present to him which will give him some say in how he is going to resolve the problem.

Guideline 12

Never compare.

We are all running our own race. Everyone has his own strengths and weaknesses, which is why comparing your child to other children is unfair.

Praise
Appreciation
Individuality
Celebration
Encouragement

Description

It's tough to never compare your child to a sibling or friend. At the very least, though, we need to minimize our comparisons. And it's very important not to vocalize them within hearing range of your child. When you compare your child with another, you quit appreciating your child for who she is.

A Great Example

I had a student who was an amazing athlete. This young lady was an Olympic caliber martial artist. For several years, she was the number one competitor in the country in her age group. She spent her teen years traveling and competing both nationally and internationally. This girl was born to win. Besides being a great athlete, she had a wonderful personality and a great attitude. Everyone liked her and wanted to be around her.

This young lady had a little sister three years her junior. I couldn't help but feel a little sorry for kid sister. She had serious shoes to fill. Amazingly, little sister seemed to show no resentment toward her older sibling. In fact, she was her sister's biggest fan. And I think I know why.

Her parents never compared her to her older sister. They never expected her to do the same things. They constantly affirmed her and recognized her unique gifts. One time, after my student had just won an event, I saw the family interacting and I went up to talk to them. I praised my student for another win and made some comment to her parents about how they should be proud of their daughter. Without missing a beat, her father said, "We are. We're proud of both our girls. They are both amazing in their own way." He did so while smiling and making eye contact with his youngest daughter.

At that moment, I understood why she didn't feel any jealousy towards her big sister. There was no need to. Her family loved and affirmed her for who she was. Karate champion or not, it didn't matter to her parents. They loved her just the same.

Room for Improvement

A man wanted to enroll his two young boys in martial arts. I was absolutely stunned by how he introduced his boys to me.

He said, "This is Toby. He's twelve years old and a great athlete. He also is an excellent student. As a matter of fact, he's pretty good at everything he does. And this is my youngest son, Nick. He's eight years old. He's not nearly the athlete his big brother is. I'm kind of worried about him because he's not very bright either. We're doing our best to have him try to be more like his big brother."

I looked over at little Nick as his father was describing him and he sadly nodded in agreement. I could almost hear him thinking, "It must be true, right? I mean, my dad wouldn't lie, would he?"

Never in my life had I witnessed such a blatant comparison. I knew this dad loved both his boys, but he sure had a strange way of showing it. I pulled the father aside during the boys' orientation class to address the issue. I explained to him how damaging I felt the public comparison was that he had just made about his boys. Surprisingly, he was more receptive than I thought he would be. As a matter of fact, he thanked me and then enrolled both boys in our program right then. Both boys ended up training with me for years and earned their black belts.

Years later, I received a thank you letter from the father expressing how beneficial martial arts had been for both his boys. He also went on to say what a big impact our initial conversation had made on how he practices parenting. He told me that it had never felt right to compare his two boys, but that was what his father had done with him and his brother. He just thought that it was what parents did.

I doubt that anyone reading this book has compared their child to someone else as blatantly as this father did. With that said, it is probably not a bad idea to be mindfully aware of any comparisons that you do make.

Tool 12: When you catch yourself comparing your child to others, stop immediately and ask yourself, "How can I help her run his own race?"

Guideline 13

Maintain *rigid flexibility*.

Maintaining *rigid flexibility* means being more concerned with the spirit of the family rules versus the actual rules themselves. It means to set a high standard for your child, while knowing that there are going to be exceptions to this standard. That's just life. In an attempt to parent well, we sometimes rigidly adhere to a rule when it doesn't make sense.

Rigid flexibility is like a willow tree in the wind. It's flexible enough to bend. Otherwise, it would break. When a situation arises in which it's obvious that being flexible is the wise decision for the greater good, we can bend.

Guidelines are very useful, but every parent needs to "call an inaudible" from time to time. In other words, there are times when you will need to decide what to do at the last second after weighing all the possible options.

Flexibility
Balance
Responsiveness
Standards
Innovation

Description

Coach John Wooden, the legendary college basketball coach, had a specific way of working with his players. He believed in treating them the same by treating them differently. He didn't demand the same things from every player. He looked at them as individuals and then adjusted his expectations accordingly. This is the concept behind **rigid flexibility**.

Parents often have a difficult time with rigid flexibility because they view it as being inconsistent. **Rigid flexibility** is really about balance. Some parents are too flexible with their children. They let them have way too much freedom and let them make way too many decisions on their own. Other parents are the exact opposite. They make all of the decisions for their children and they adhere to their parenting principles to a fault, never allowing for any flexibility.

The beauty of **rigid flexibility** is that it helps you to develop a set of clear guidelines that your child understands. Do your best to stick to them, but know that these guidelines won't always fit and will need to be bent a little as the situation requires.

A Great Example

I learned to maintain rigid flexibility from my older brother, Tim. We do black belt testing three times a year in our martial arts schools, a process which has been developed and formalized over thirty years of trial and error. We are very strict on the test dates. For example, if you can't make the April test dates, then you simply have to reschedule for August. We do this because we found that, if we're the least bit flexible, we end up fielding all kinds of unrealistic requests for customized belt tests.

Several years back, we were approached by a family regarding their black belt tests. Being Seventh-day Adventists, they celebrated the Sabbath on Saturdays and could not, in good conscience, test that day.

I went to talk this over with Tim in order to formulate the proper response to this family. I was sure that he would help me find the words to explain to them the importance of coming on Saturday to test. Instead, Tim looked me in the eye and said, "Why don't we do a special test for them on

Thursday night? We can't in good conscience expect them to do something incongruent with their beliefs, can we?" It seemed so logical once he said it, but I had been so ingrained in my belief pattern that the thought never occurred to me. We ended up having a Thursday test. The family did great and everyone left happy.

Room for Improvement

In order for school-age students testing to be promoted from one rank to another in our martial arts schools, they have to show proof that they are doing well at home and in school. We do this by sending an **Intent to Promote** form home with them. They have to bring it back with signatures and approval from both their teacher and their parents.

From time to time, a child will return the form with a note from his teacher saying he is not doing well at school. When this happens, we work with the family to devise a plan of action. Most of the time, a note from the child's teacher saying that he is trying hard and moving in the right direction is enough for us to continue on with the belt promotion. The parents nearly always agree with us.

One of our students was struggling at school. He had been diagnosed with a learning disorder and, as a result, not only were his grades weak but he suffered from behavior issues, as well. He was pretty good for us while he was in class. His parents said that our class was the only place where he seemed to learn.

When his **Intent to Promote** form was returned to us, it was obvious that his grades weren't what they should be. I spoke with the parents about having his teacher send us a note indicating that he was improving, as that would be good enough for us. We didn't want to hold him back too long because we didn't want him to lose interest in martial arts. After all, martial arts was doing him a great deal of good and it seemed to be the only thing working for him.

The boy's dad refused to budge. He remained inflexible as he saw this as an opportunity to strong-arm his child to get better grades. He was the dad and I had to support his decision, but I was concerned about the effects. Once this child realized that his belt promotion was months away instead of just days, he completely lost interest in his martial arts training and the family drifted off. I can't help but think that if his father would've applied the concept of **rigid flexibility**, we could have been a strong ally in helping this child navigate through this rough time.

Tool 13: Decide where you are on the *Rigid Flexibility* pendulum. If you feel you are either too lenient or too strict, make adjustments.

Guideline 14

Don't speak out of anger.

We are all emotional beings and we tend to be more emotional with our children, in both good ways and bad ways, because we love and care for them so much. It is for this reason that we need to be extra mindful of our emotions when we are dealing with them.

Sometimes, our fuse is pretty short when we're under a lot of pressure—going through a divorce, hitting a rough patch at work, or experiencing relationship, money or health problems. Something your child did which, normally, might be mildly irksome might trigger a violent inner reaction during these times.

Make certain that you are not taking your anger and frustration with yourself or your situation out on your child. When you let your anger rip, it does a lot of damage...some of which might be irreparable. This is why it's so vital to practice not speaking out of anger.

Awareness

Self-control

Calm

Mindfulness

Logic

Patience

Silence

Description

One heated argument or one angry sentence is oftentimes all it takes to drive a wedge between you and your child. Do your best to avoid this situation at all costs. Try not to speak out of anger. It is natural to lose your temper from time to time, but beware of what you say when you lose your self-control. If you don't watch your words, chances are they will come back to bite you later.

Some circumstances might demand that you raise your voice to your child. However, there is a difference between raising your voice to your child because you need to get his attention and yelling at him because you lose your temper. If you lose your temper and end up saying things in the heat of the moment, you'll regret it.

Yes, you can apologize to your child and you should, but saying something out of anger and then apologizing for it later is like pounding a nail into a wall. The apology might remove the nail from the wall, but the nail's hole remains. It is far better not to say anything in the first place for which you might have to apologize later.

The concept of self-control when we get angry is easy to talk about but extremely hard to put into practice. The first step is awareness. Notice when you are beginning to get angry. When you're aware of your anger, you will be able to objectify it. And what you can objectify, you can better control. Even though you're angry, this awareness will help you respond to the situation more logically. At the very least, this awareness might be all you need to keep your mouth shut until the wave of anger has passed.

A Great Example

One of the highlights of raising my kids is going up to our family cabin. Wintertime, summertime, early spring...it doesn't matter. We all love it there. It's especially enjoyable when we share our cabin with friends. On one particular trip, our friends came up in a new jet black SUV. Kyle, the father, had wanted this truck for years. It had all the bells and whistles and he was jazzed.

The following afternoon, our two sons were racing their bikes around the neighborhood. When the lunchtime bell rang, they sprinted towards the cabin, both vying to be the first back. Kyle's son, Jesse, misjudged his speed and had to swerve at the last minute to avoid hitting his little sister. Unfortunately, he ran smack dab into the side of his father's brand new truck. No one was hurt, but the scratch was too big to be buffed out.

Jesse felt terrible. He knew how his dad felt about that truck and, in his child mind, he had ruined it forever. I'm not sure how I would've handled it with my son if he had scratched my new truck, but I can only hope that I would handle it as well as Kyle did.

Kyle quickly saw it for what it was...an accident. I could tell that Kyle was angry, at first. It would have been easy for him to make Jesse feel even worse by scolding him, but he didn't. I could almost hear him thinking that his son's self-esteem was worth more than his brand new truck.

Kyle looked at Jesse and asked him if he was all right. Then he told him, "No worries, buddy. I know you didn't mean to do it. It's okay. We can get the truck fixed next week." They hugged. It took Jesse a few minutes to regain his composure. I looked on with a new appreciation for Kyle's parenting skills and his ability to respond with love rather than with anger.

Room for Improvement

My daughter is an extremely happy young lady. She was born that way. If there's an exception, it's when she's choosing her outfit for the day every morning before school.

I'm not sure why this happens. The night before, she will have narrowed down the next day's attire to four choices. But when morning rolls around none of these outfits work for her. Sometimes this makes her grumpy.

One morning I had had enough. I had a lot to do at work that day and we were going to be late if she didn't decide on the right color socks to wear. Pretty quickly, I lost it. I don't remember exactly what I said, but it wasn't pretty.

Looking back on that moment now, it's hard to believe that I had thought that yelling at her would help. To the contrary, she was slower than ever and the following five minutes were miserable for everyone.

Things were tense during the ride to school that morning. Still angry, I vented, saying some things to my daughter that I still regret. Of course, later on that afternoon I apologized. But I could not erase my comments from her memory. This is why it's so important we don't speak out of anger. These aren't the kind of memories we want to create for our children.

Tool 14: Focus on one thing your child does that makes you angry. Keep it simple. For example, you might get angry when he leaves his dirty clothes on the floor. Mindfully decide to talk to him in a logical fashion about this issue.

When you are able to be calm about the small things, you can deal with bigger issues. Next time you find yourself angry with your child over that bigger issue, do your best to take care of the immediate situation as needed while saying as little as possible. Once you calm down, go back and talk to him.

Guideline 15

★

Make sure your child knows that you love her unconditionally.

The most important thing you can do as a parent is to let your child know—by your words and your actions—that you love her unconditionally.

Affection

Engagement

Communication

Creativity

Constancy

Description

Loving your child unconditionally is an innate response for most parents and something most of us would never question. However, parents are often so busy with their daily demands that they forget to communicate their unconditional love to their child.

Nothing helps your child to feel more loved and appreciated than spending quality time with her. Create and seize opportunities to spend one-on-one time with your child, other than watching television. Engage with her, whichever activity you choose.

There are many ways to express your unconditional love for your child. In fact, the more you do this, the more ways you'll find to show your unconditional love.

Tell your child, "I love you," on a regular basis. For some parents, this is difficult. Do it anyway. Tell your child first thing in the morning, last thing at night, during an argument, after an argument... It doesn't matter exactly when you tell her. Just make sure you tell her.

There is so much you can do to let your child know that you love her! You can write her a note and put it in an unsuspected place—on the bathroom mirror in the morning, in her lunch bag or on her pillow. Or you can make something for your child—breakfast in bed, a handmade toy or a scrapbook of her last soccer season.

Finally, be there for your child when she needs you. We all fall down at times. You show your unconditional love when you are there to pick your child up regardless of what made her fall down.

A Great Example

The Shepherd's had four boys, all bunched together in a 7-year time span. All four of these young men were "all boy." They were extremely physical, energetic and a bit mischievous. We affectionately referred to them as "the storm." They weren't bad, but they got into their fair share of trouble. Regardless of what happened, their parents were always there for them.

Being there for their sons didn't mean that they bailed them out of trouble or let them go unpunished. They practiced tough love. They made sure that their boys felt the consequences of their actions. With that said, their parents were always able to communicate to their boys that they loved them regardless of what they did. I remember one particular incident where the oldest boy was caught egging a neighbors car. His father asked me if I would join forces with him in discussing the ramifications of his actions. He felt my influence in the matter would help to redirect his son's energy in the future. I was happy to oblige and the two of us met with his oldest son.

I'll never forget the father's opening sentence to his son. He looked him in the eye and said, "You know I love you, son. I'll always love you no matter what you do, but this behavior is unacceptable." We determined the consequences for his actions on the spot. There were quite a few and, thankfully, the boy stepped up and did what he was asked to do to make the situation right.

Recently, I had a discussion with this young man about the incident. He commented that, although his father was pretty strict with the boys growing up, he needed to be. He said that they always knew that they were loved and that this unconditional love helped him become the kind of person he wanted to be.

Room for Improvement

My daughter's kindergarten class took a field trip to Angel Island near San Francisco. Near the end of the day, some of the children (and parents) were getting a bit cranky. It had been a long afternoon. Everyone was hungry and the thought of driving home in heavy traffic had brought everyone back to reality.

One girl in particular was having a bit of a meltdown. I don't remember what the tantrum was about, but I certainly remember her dad's response. He looked at her and said, "If you don't stop whining, I'm going to leave you here to fend for yourself. There are plenty of other little girls who would appreciate your bedroom and your toys."

I wasn't the only parent who heard those comments. Several of us looked at each other in stunned disbelief, even though we knew that he didn't really mean what he said and that he was only trying to get his daughter's attention. She became hysterical and cried buckets. It took another mom quite awhile to calm her down.

I still get angry when I think about it. Put yourself in that little girl's shoes and imagine how it must have felt to have your father so ready to trade you in! Did she feel unconditionally loved? Not likely. We've all been angry with our children before. We might have even said some things we shouldn't have. But let's remember never to give our children a reason to think that we don't love them unconditionally.

Tool 15: At least once a week, do something completely random to show your child that you love her unconditionally. If you need to, calendar it into your phone, write yourself a note and stick it on your dashboard, etc. to make sure you remember.

Why Your Child Needs Martial Arts

THE BENEFITS OF ENROLLING YOUR CHILD in a martial arts program extend far beyond self-defense. Martial arts will help your child in nearly every aspect of her life. It will improve your child's health, fitness, athletic abilities, confidence, concentration and behavior.

Does this sound too good to be true? It's not. Many experts agree that martial arts are good medicine for the escalating childhood obesity, increased violence at school, and deterioration of the family structure.

There is a reason why Dr. Phil, Jillian Michaels (expert from the television show, *The Biggest Loser*), Tony Robbins, pediatricians, child physiologists and educators the world over all recommend martial arts as one of the most svaluable activities in which your child can participate.

Confidence *Composure*
Health *Control*
Fitness *Respect*
Strength *Self-defense*
Flexibility *Safety*
Endurance *Success*
Athleticism *Achievement*
Balance *Goals*
Peace

The Benefits of Martial Arts

Self-Defense. The self-defense benefits of martial arts could be described as practice the fight so that you don't have to. As your child trains he will become more confident in his ability to defend himself. As this confidence increases the need to defend himself will decrease naturally because he will begin to carry himself in a more confident manner. He'll project confidence to everyone around him and will be less vulnerable to predatory behavior. Martial arts training includes strategic or preventative self-defense as well as physical self-defense. Your child will learn how to recognize potentially dangerous situations and how to avoid confrontations.

Athletic Enhancement. There is a reason why every professional sports team in every major sport supplements their training with martial arts. Martial arts training offers several advantages. It is amazingly effective in enhancing general coordination because it uses every part of the body in a balanced way. Upper body, lower body, right side, left side, forward movement, lateral movement and rotational movement are all included in martial arts training.

Fitness. Fitness has three components: strength, flexibility and endurance. Martial arts training demands a balance between the three. Therefore, a child who trains in martial arts will find her weakest areas greatly improved. Because of her greater balance of strength, flexibility and endurance your child will be less likely to injure herself while participating in other athletic activities.

Health. While martial arts training improves health for people of all ages, it is especially effective for children. It's great exercise and it's fun so kids don't mind doing it. And part of martial arts training includes discussing diet and lifestyle habits so children who grow up training develop healthy habits that stick with them for life.

Concentration. Very few activities engage the mind, body and spirit more than martial arts. Because of this a child's ability to concentrate is greatly enhanced by his martial arts training. He'll bring this ability to concentrate to other activities, too.

Respect and Courtesy. Martial arts techniques are, by nature, designed to injure others when applied. Because of this, martial arts instructors greatly stress the importance of respect, courtesy and restraint. It has been proven time and again that children who are skilled in martial arts tend to be extremely respectful, considerate and composed.

Confidence. Martial arts training always increases a child's confidence for two specific reasons. First, there are no bench sitters. Every child participates and competes against her own potential rather than against the other students. Second, martial arts training is built on the concept of setting your child up for success by giving her a series of realistic, short-term goals that she can attain quickly while keeping her focused on an exciting long-term goal. Each time she experiences success her confidence improves until she begins to believe that she can accomplish just about anything with hard work and dedication.

Keeping It Simple

MORE AN ART THAN A SCIENCE, raising children is both challenging and incredibly rewarding. Each child comes into this world with his own agenda. Oftentimes our children throw curves at us that we never saw coming and, when that happens, it is hard to know exactly what to do.

I'm reminded of a story I once heard about a famous landscape architect, a master. He traveled the world creating amazing gardens and landscapes at prestigious locations. On days when he felt particularly challenged, he would pull out a mysterious piece of paper from his pocket, glance at it, nod, fold it back up and get to work with renewed inspiration and energy, resulting in another masterpiece. People were astounded by his brilliant designs that would seem to appear from thin air after he studied that piece of paper.

Eventually, the master died. His curious colleagues approached his widow and asked to see that mysterious piece of paper as they were convinced it contained the secret to his success.

After much to-do, she allowed them one glance at the old slip of paper. As they gathered around, she carefully unfolded the paper. They looked at the writing. It simply said, "When laying sod, always put the green side up."

I love this story! It reminds me how easy it is to overcomplicate things, especially parenting. In my experience, the answers to most parenting challenges are in these *HealthierKids, SmarterKids*. We only have to remember to call upon them in times of need.

I hope you'll find *HealthierKids, SmarterKids* to be a valuable resource for years to come.

Dave Kovar

TAUGHT BY HIS PARENTS TO HAVE RESPECT for health and fitness at an early age, Dave Kovar has spent his adult life perfecting his approach to better physical, mental and emotional fitness.

A father of two, Dave holds the rank of black belt in ten different martial arts disciplines. In one of those disciplines, he has achieved a seventh-degree, which has earned him the title of "Kyoshi."

Dave Kovar is known in the martial arts world as the "Teacher's Teacher." Since 1978, Dave has helped over 25,000 students of all ages develop their character and fitness through martial arts instruction through his *Kovar Satori Academy of Martial Arts* schools and the hundreds of martial arts schools with which he has consulted. Over the years, Dave has carefully developed a system that helps his students apply the mental aspects of martial arts to excel in many areas of their lives.

The Martial Arts Industry Association (MAIA) presented Dave with its "2010 Lifetime Achievement Award" in recognition of his teaching abilities. This prestigious award has also been won by Chuck Norris and other martial arts luminaries. In 1992, the United States Martial Arts Association (USMA) honored Dave as its "Martial Arts Instructor of the Year."

Dave Kovar continues to break new ground with innovations in the martial arts industry, including fitness, nutrition and character development. Revered for being a successful businessman, Dave is also a highly respected authority in optimizing personal fulfillment and in peak performance.

Made in the USA
Charleston, SC
10 November 2012